MONSTER MANIA

WEREWOLVES

John Malam

QEB

QEB Publishing

Illustrator: Vincent Boulanger
Editor: Amanda Askew
Designer: Matthew Kelly
Picture Researcher: Maria Joannou

Published in the United States by
QEB Publishing, Inc.
3 Wrigley, Suite A
Irvine, CA 92618

www.qed-publishing.co.uk

Library of Congress Cataloging-in-Publication Data

Malam, John, 1957-
Werewolves / John Malam.
p. cm. -- (QEB Monster mania)
Includes bibliographical references and index.
ISBN 978-1-59566-748-9 (library binding : alk. paper)
1. Werewolves--Juvenile literature. I. Title.
GR830.W4M33 2011
398.24'54--dc22

2010008527

Printed in China

Words in **bold** can be found in the Glossary on page 31.

Acknowledgments

Alamy Images Photos 12/Archives du 7eme Art 8, Universal Images Group
Limited 25r, Pictorial Press Ltd 30; **Corbis** Images.com 5; **DK Images** Steve
Gorton 13t; **Getty Images** Hulton Archive/Stringer 28b, The Bridgeman Art
Library 29b; Istockphoto/David Naylor 20; **Mary Evans Picture Library** 17r;
Photolibrary AlaskaStock 17l; **Photoshot** Universal Pictures/Starstock 21b; **Rex
Features** Universal/Everett 9, Everett Collection 12; **Shutterstock** Olemac 15b,
S.M. 16l, Rickshu 16r, Martin Muránsky 24, Wheatley 25l, Marcelo Dufflocq W.
28t, Steve Mann 29t; **Topham Picturepoint** 21t, Anthony Wallis/Fortean Picture
Library 13b

CONTENTS

A world of werewolves   4

Who's who among werewolves?   5

The Very First Werewolf   6

How werewolves are made   8

Little Red Riding Hood   10

How to spot a werewolf   12

An American Werewolf   14

Howling at the Moon   16

Peter Stubbe, Werewolf of Bedburg   18

Powers of werewolves   20

Werewolves of Greifswald   22

Protection from werewolves   24

Jean Grenier, a Teenage Werewolf   26

How to slay a werewolf   28

Timeline   30

Glossary   31

Index   32

A WORLD OF WEREWOLVES

According to old **folk stories**, werewolves are human beings who change their shape into wolflike creatures. They become savage monsters that hunt, attack, bite, and kill.

Werewolves are creatures of the night, but as the darkness fades away and daylight returns, they shift their shapes back into human form. Werewolves lead double lives, hiding inside their human hosts.

But, when werewolf attacks are suspected, panic sets in. Long ago, in parts of Europe, hunters tracked down werewolves, trials were held, and people thought to be these monsters were put to death.

Meaning of werewolf

The word "werewolf" is made from the Old English word "wer," which means "man," added to the word "wolf." It literally means "man-wolf."

A scratch from a werewolf was said to be enough to cause a person to change from human to wolf.

WHO'S WHO
AMONG WEREWOLVES?

FAIRYTALE WEREWOLVES

In fairy tales there is sometimes a creature described as a "big, bad wolf." For example, in the well-known tale of *Little Red Riding Hood*, an old woman disappears and a wicked wolf takes her place. In other words, the old woman has **shape-shifted** from a human into a wolf, and that means she is a werewolf.

AND THE REST

VOLUNTARY WEREWOLVES

These are people who, for whatever reason, actually want to become werewolves. They are the opposite of involuntary werewolves.

IMAGINARY WEREWOLVES

These are people who think they are werewolves. The truth is they are ordinary humans with vivid imaginations.

INVOLUNTARY WEREWOLVES

These are people who never set out to become werewolves, but when something happened to them, they were changed into monsters.

The Very First
WEREWOLF

It's hard to be certain where werewolves came from, but one of the first stories was told by the people of ancient Greece, about 2,500 years ago.

There was once a king called Lycaon (say: *lie-kay-on*) who ruled over Arcadia, a region of Greece. He was not a religious man, and this made the gods angry. Zeus, the king of the gods, decided to visit Lycaon to find out what sort of a person he was.

Zeus disguised himself as a peasant, and asked Lycaon for food and shelter. Lycaon had a feeling he was being tricked. A banquet was prepared, but instead of feeding his guest with animal meat, Lycaon served him human flesh. If the stranger was indeed a god, he would be disgusted by such vile meat.

The great god Zeus came down to Earth to discover if King Lycaon was a good or a bad person.

Werewolf for nine years

There is another version of this story. It says that every time a sacrifice was made at Lycaon's altar, a man was turned into a wolf. After nine years, the werewolf changed back into human form – but only if it had not eaten human flesh. If it had tasted human meat, it would remain a werewolf forever.

When Zeus saw the food, he knew that Lycaon was indeed a bad person. He threw the table over, and hurled bolts of lightning at Lycaon's sons, killing them all, except one.

Zeus hurled his lightning bolts with deadly accuracy.

As for Lycaon, Zeus dealt him a punishment far worse than death. He turned him into a wolf, for only a wolf would enjoy the taste of human flesh.

Werewolves are lycanthropes

A werewolf can also be called a **lycanthrope**. This comes from two Greek words – *lykos* meaning 'wolf', and *anthropos* meaning 'human'.

Lycaon's fate was sealed, and he became the first werewolf.

7

How WEREWOLVES are made

According to stories, there are two ways for a human to become a werewolf. The person either wants to change into a werewolf, or the person is a victim and tries to resist—but they cannot stop the shape-shifting process.

I WANT TO BE A WEREWOLF

People who want to be werewolves are voluntary werewolves. They rub ointment made from herbs on their body, chant spells, tie belts of wolfskin around their waist, and cover themselves with wolf pelts. Some werewolves claim to have been transformed by sipping water from the paw print of a wolf, or by sleeping in a wolf's lair. These people think they have been transformed, and for a time they act as if they are wolves.

The human body changes to one covered in thick fur with wolflike claws and teeth.

I DON'T WANT TO BE A WEREWOLF

People who do not want to be werewolves are involuntary werewolves. For them, it might start with a scratch or a bite from a werewolf, and when this happens, their fate is sealed. In some stories, a person becomes a werewolf when a sorcerer curses them, or a magician casts a spell on them.

Once the process of **transformation** from human to werewolf begins, nothing can stop it (*An American Werewolf in London*, 1981).

The wolf belt

Many old stories, especially ones from northern Europe, talk about **wolf belts**. Made from strips of wolfskin, they were said to work like lucky charms. When a person wore a wolf belt, they felt as if they had a wolf's strength.

Little Red RIDING HOOD

Once upon a time, there was a little girl who lived near a forest. Whenever she went out, she wore a bright-red riding cloak, so people called her Little Red Riding Hood.

One day, she set out to visit her grandmother, whose cottage was among the trees. On the way she met a wolf, who asked her where she was going. No sooner had she replied, than the wolf ran away.

The wolf went to the grandmother's house, and knocked on the door. Thinking it was Little Red Riding Hood, the old lady opened the door—and the wolf leapt upon her and gobbled her up. The wolf got dressed in the grandmother's clothes, and climbed into her bed.

Little Red Riding Hood was shocked to see the wolf.

When Little Red Riding Hood arrived, she said,
    "What big ears you have!"
    "All the better to hear you with, my dear," replied the wolf.
    "What big teeth you have!" said Little Red
Riding Hood.
    "All the better to eat you with!" roared the
wolf, jumping onto Little Red Riding Hood
and swallowing her up.

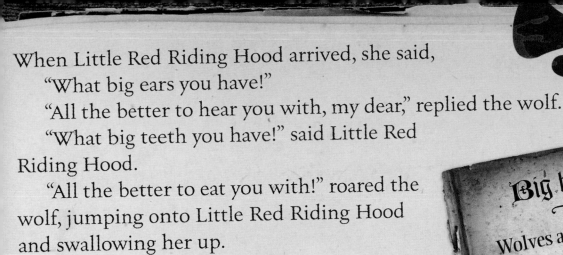

Big bad wolf

Wolves are the baddies in many fairy tales. In The Wolf and the Seven Young Kids, a hungry wolf eats seven baby goats, which are eventually set free unharmed. In The Three Little Pigs, a wolf is killed by a pig, but not until the wolf has tried to eat the pigs.

The hunter set Little Red Riding Hood and her grandmother free.

This story comes from
FRANCE and
GERMANY

A short while later, a hunter passed by and saw the wolf. He knew it must have eaten the old lady, so the hunter took a pair of scissors and cut open the wolf's belly. Out climbed Little Red Riding Hood and her grandmother. Then they packed stones into the wolf's body and sewed up the cut. When the wolf woke, it was so heavy it could hardly move, and it dropped down dead.

11

How to spot a WEREWOLF

Stories say that werewolves lead double lives. In the daytime they appear in their human form, but at night they are transformed into savage beasts.

A WEREWOLF IN HUMAN FORM

At first sight, a werewolf in its unchanged form looks like a normal human. But if the person seems nervous or restless, then a werewolf might be lurking inside.

Other important clues are eyebrows that come together on the bridge of the nose, long, curved fingernails, and canine or biting teeth that seem long and sharp, more like a large dog's or a wolf's than a human's.

There can be no doubt that this is the face of a werewolf, not a human.

Sign of the werewolf

According to stories, werewolves are marked with a five-pointed star, or **pentagram**, usually on their chest or hand. It's always there, and when they are in their human form they cover it up.

If the person is cut, fur might be seen within the wound. Bristles might be spotted under the tongue, and beware of people who have fur on the palms of their hands. None of these features is right for a human, so it must mean there is an animal hiding inside the person.

Human fingers are transformed into animal claws.

A WEREWOLF IN WEREWOLF FORM

A fully transformed werewolf doesn't look anything like a wolf. It is bigger, and while an ordinary wolf has a tail, a werewolf never does. It walks upright on two legs, not on all fours. Its eyes are fiery red and its fur has a silvery sheen. If the creature speaks with a human voice, then it can only be a werewolf.

A werewolf always walks on two legs, rather than four like a wolf.

You are a werewolf!

The biggest clue of all to spotting a werewolf is this: an injury to a werewolf will show up in exactly the same place on its human body. So, if a werewolf is cut on the left leg, there will be an identical cut in the same place on its human leg.

13

An American WEREWOLF

People from Europe who settled in North America took werewolf stories with them, and soon America had its own stories of man-wolves.

Snydertown is a small town in Pennsylvania. The townsfolk became suspicious of an old man who lived on his own and didn't mix with other people. He was often seen visiting the farm of Mr. and Mrs. Paul, watching their daughter, May, as she looked after the family's sheep.

This story comes from **Pennsylvania**

The creepy old man watched May Paul as she tended to the sheep.

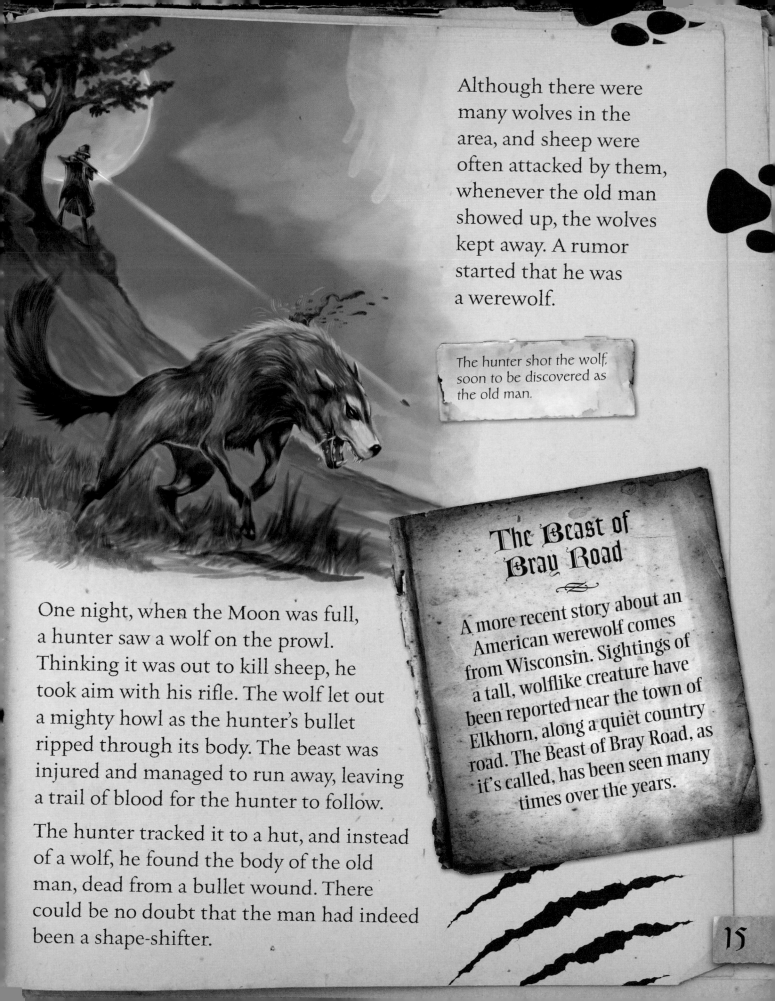

Although there were many wolves in the area, and sheep were often attacked by them, whenever the old man showed up, the wolves kept away. A rumor started that he was a werewolf.

The hunter shot the wolf, soon to be discovered as the old man.

One night, when the Moon was full, a hunter saw a wolf on the prowl. Thinking it was out to kill sheep, he took aim with his rifle. The wolf let out a mighty howl as the hunter's bullet ripped through its body. The beast was injured and managed to run away, leaving a trail of blood for the hunter to follow.

The hunter tracked it to a hut, and instead of a wolf, he found the body of the old man, dead from a bullet wound. There could be no doubt that the man had indeed been a shape-shifter.

The Beast of Bray Road

A more recent story about an American werewolf comes from Wisconsin. Sightings of a tall, wolflike creature have been reported near the town of Elkhorn, along a quiet country road. The Beast of Bray Road, as it's called, has been seen many times over the years.

HOWLING AT THE MOON

Since ancient times the Moon has been linked to strange events on Earth. When there's a full Moon in the sky, it's werewolf night. According to folk tales, it's the Moon that brings these shape-shifters out, changing humans into howling monsters.

The changing shape of the Moon has become linked with the transformation of man into monster.

As a full Moon rises, a werewolf emerges, ready to rampage through the night.

CHANGING SHAPE

The Moon seems to change its shape throughout the month, from a crescent to a full circle, and then fading from sight. Werewolves are said to break out of their human body during a full Moon—its power is so great it pulls the beast from its human host.

MOONLIGHT

In the past, it was thought moonlight changed people into "lunatics," which comes from *luna*, the Latin word for "moon." Even the British government believed this, and in 1842 a law was made that said people who suffered from "Moon madness" acted strangely when the Moon was full.

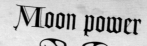

Moon power

It's not just werewolves that come out on a moonlit night. Folk tales are full of witches and fairies who are at their most active when the Moon is full, and ugly hags are transformed into beautiful maidens.

In this Victorian illustration, a werewolf pounces on a man during the night of a full Moon.

Wolves are more active on bright, moonlit nights than on dark, moonless nights.

HOWLING AT THE MOON

Werewolves and ordinary wolves are said to howl at the Moon, as if moonlight sets something off inside them. In werewolf stories, the Moon is usually a vital part of the plot, causing the transformation process to start, and the howling to begin.

Peter Stubbe, WEREWOLF OF BEDBURG

Around 400 years ago, rumors were started about a man from Bedburg, Germany, who believed he was a werewolf. This caused panic, and local people lived in fear.

The man's name was Peter Stubbe, and he was a farmer with a secret. One day, a young boy was snatched by a wolf, and when it was tracked to its lair, the hunters saw it shape-shift into human form. At that point they knew they were dealing with a werewolf—none other than Farmer Stubbe.

Hunters saw the boy had been taken by a werewolf.

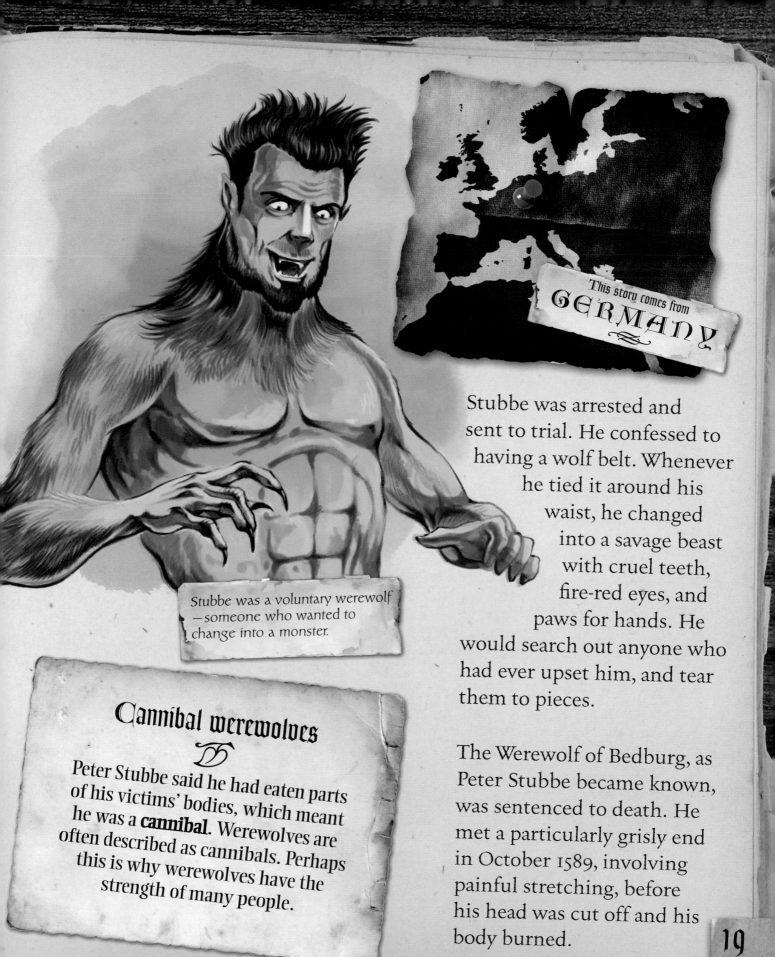

Stubbe was a voluntary werewolf—someone who wanted to change into a monster.

Cannibal werewolves

Peter Stubbe said he had eaten parts of his victims' bodies, which meant he was a **cannibal**. Werewolves are often described as cannibals. Perhaps this is why werewolves have the strength of many people.

Stubbe was arrested and sent to trial. He confessed to having a wolf belt. Whenever he tied it around his waist, he changed into a savage beast with cruel teeth, fire-red eyes, and paws for hands. He would search out anyone who had ever upset him, and tear them to pieces.

The Werewolf of Bedburg, as Peter Stubbe became known, was sentenced to death. He met a particularly grisly end in October 1589, involving painful stretching, before his head was cut off and his body burned.

19

Powers of WEREWOLVES

In pictures, artists make werewolves look as strong as possible.

Werewolves are powerful creatures. Their power is everything—without it they would be as weak as when they are human.

STRENGTH AND POWER

Stories about werewolves say that these part-human, part-animal beings have the strength of many ordinary humans. Some people think this strength comes from werewolves eating their victims. The more they eat, the stronger they get.

Wolf sense

A werewolf has the intelligence of a human. This means it can track and recognize its victims, and avoid any traps that might have been set for it.

SUPER SENSES

Werewolves are creatures of the night, with excellent powers of seeing in the dark. They also have a good sense of smell. These two senses give the monster a huge advantage over their human victims. Werewolves can easily detect humans in the dark, whereas human sight and smell will not pick up the danger until it is too late to escape.

Its keen senses of sight and smell help a werewolf to detect a victim at night.

Powerful jaws packed with sharp, biting teeth can easily tear through flesh.

CHANGING SHAPE

Werewolves have the power to change their shape from human to beast, and then back again. Each time this happens, new body tissue is formed, and there are some who say this gives werewolves the power to live forever. But, as werewolves are often discovered and killed, their lives are usually short.

21

Werewolves OF GREIFSWALD

This story was retold in a book by Jodocus Temme, who came across it in northeast Germany. It tells of a time when werewolves plagued the town of Greifswald.

Greifswald is an old town, with one of the oldest universities in Europe. It was said that werewolves had taken up residence in the center of town, and any student who dared to walk the streets after dark would be set upon by the monsters.

The citizens of Greifswald were under attack from werewolves.

Wanting to fight back, one of the students had an idea. He suggested that they should collect as much silver as they could. Buttons, buckles, goblets, jewelry, forks, and spoons were gathered and thrown into a furnace, where they were turned into liquid silver. Carefully, the liquid was molded into small balls of silver.

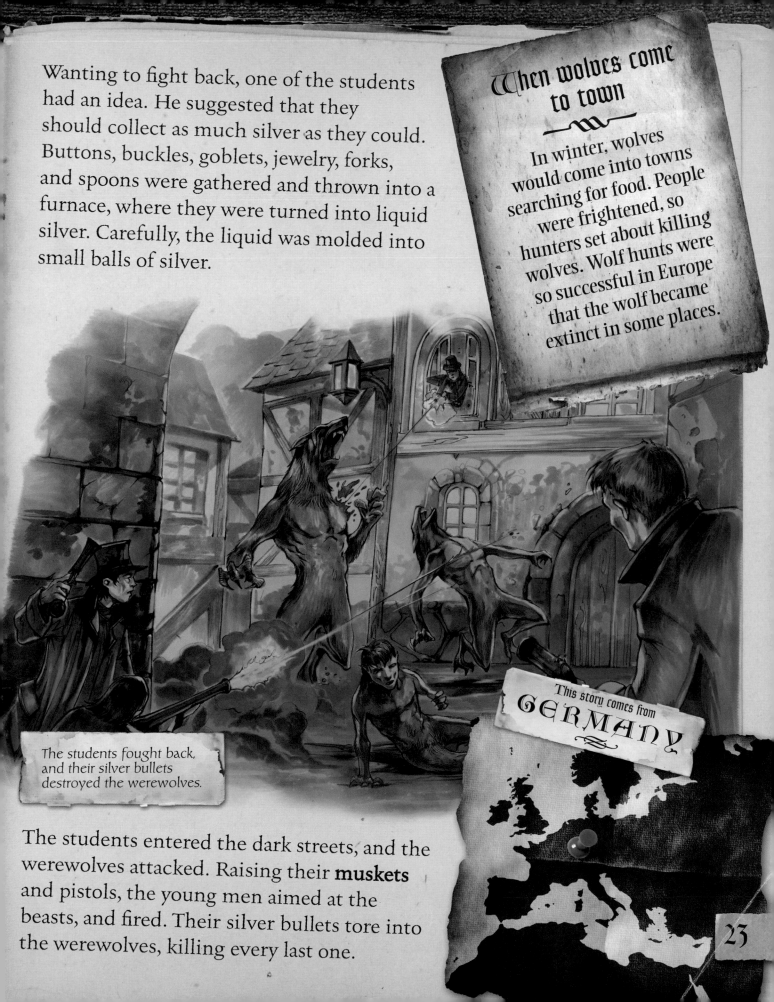

The students fought back, and their silver bullets destroyed the werewolves.

This story comes from
GERMANY

The students entered the dark streets, and the werewolves attacked. Raising their **muskets** and pistols, the young men aimed at the beasts, and fired. Their silver bullets tore into the werewolves, killing every last one.

Protection from WEREWOLVES

Werewolves are usually described as tough creatures without any fear. Once they've moved into an area, there's very little that can be done to keep them away.

STAY INDOORS

The best protection is to never go outside when it is a full Moon, and stay well away from forests where werewolves might lurk.

ODD BEHAVIOR

Anyone could be a werewolf in disguise. Nervous, fidgety behavior, unexplained cuts and bruises, and a constant thirst are all signs of a possible shape-shifter, and the person would be avoided, especially at full Moon.

It was thought that silver was protection against werewolves. People kept silver objects in their homes, and carried silver coins with them.

PRAYING TO THE GODS

Prayers were offered to Diana, the ancient goddess of wild animals and the Moon. Her magic was thought to keep werewolves away. People also prayed to St. Hubert, the patron saint of hunting. It was believed he could cure rabies, a deadly disease that passed to humans from wolves and dogs. If St Hubert could do this, then perhaps he could also offer protection from werewolves.

People prayed to Diana, goddess of the Moon, for protection against werewolves.

Superstitious people grew wolfsbane in their garden. This plant was believed to repel (banish) wolves.

CASTING SPELLS

Spells were also said, and whoever cast the spell dripped oil into a candle flame to make the magic work.

Werewolf cures

In parts of Germany, it was said that a werewolf could be cured if it was called three times by its human name. In Denmark, shouting at a werewolf, as if it was nothing more than a large, bad dog, was thought to turn it back into its human form.

25

Jean Grenier, A TEENAGE WEREWOLF

Jean Grenier, a teenage boy from France, was almost put to death in 1603 because he believed he was a werewolf.

In the courtroom, 14-year-old Jean told the most amazing tale. Three years before, he had met the Master of the Forest. This evil being scratched Jean, then gave him magic ointment for his skin and a wolfskin cloak. When he wore the cloak, he was transformed into a werewolf.

Dressed in wolfskin, Jean Grenier imagined he was a werewolf.

Jean was neither shy nor embarrassed by what he said he had done. As a werewolf he had frightened people, some of whom he claimed to have attacked and eaten. The boy was found guilty and was sentenced to be hanged.

The judge pronounced the death sentence on the teenager who claimed to be a werewolf.

It's all in the mind

Johann Weyer (c.1515–1588), a doctor from the Netherlands, was one of the first people to ask if werewolves were real or not. He said they came from people's imaginations. It was a long time before his idea was accepted.

While Jean was in prison awaiting his fate, his case was looked at in more detail. It turned out that no one had been reported missing, and no victims of wolf attacks had been found. The court decided that Jean Grenier had made everything up, looking for attention. He was sent to a monastery, where he spent the rest of his life.

How to slay a
WEREWOLF

For those who believed in werewolves, the ultimate challenge was knowing how to destroy them. The first task was always to identify the werewolf, which was difficult when the werewolf was in its human form.

DESTROYING THE HUMAN FORM

In the past, once a person was arrested on suspicion of being a werewolf, they were forced to confess their crimes, often under painful torture.

Their bodies were searched for clues, such as a cut in the same place where a wolf had been injured. Some were sent for trial, and most were found guilty. The punishment was death, either by beheading or burning at the stake.

People accused of being werewolves were put to death.

DESTROYING THE WEREWOLF FORM

There is only one way to slay a werewolf in its monster form—shooting it with a silver bullet. This precious metal was believed to have a power that could defeat evil.

As soon as a silver bullet burst into a werewolf's body, the creature would die, killing its human form, too.

In folk stories, the only sure way of destroying a werewolf is by shooting it with silver bullets—no other metal will do.

The Beast of Gévaudan

In 1764, a monstrous wolf terrorized the region of Gévaudan, France. Many people thought it was a werewolf. A local farmer, Jean Chastel, killed the Beast of Gévaudan with silver bullets. This may be where the idea of killing werewolves with silver bullets comes from.

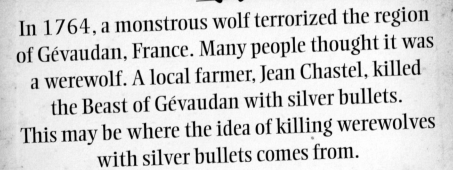

TIMELINE

1000s The word "werewulf" was first written down in English.

1039–1101 Life of Vseslav of Polotsk, a Russian prince described in folk stories as a werewolf.

1490s Trials were held in Switzerland of women accused of riding wolves.

1520–1630 In France, as many as 30,000 people were accused of being werewolves.

1521 Three men from Poligny, France, were found guilty of being werewolves and were burned at the stake.

1525–1589 Life of Peter Stubbe, who was found guilty of being a werewolf and was executed.

1603 Jean Grenier, a teenage boy from France, claimed he was a werewolf.

1640s A pack of werewolves was said to have plagued the town of Greifswald, Germany.

1697 The folk story *Little Red Riding Hood* was first written down.

1764 A large wolf, thought by some people to be a werewolf, terrorized the region of Gévaudan, France.

1913 The first werewolf movie was made, called *The Werewolf*. It was 18 minutes long, and was a silent movie.

1941 *The Wolf Man* was released, one of the most famous werewolf movies ever made.

1981 Two famous werewolf movies came out, *The Howling* and *An American Werewolf in London*.
An American Werewolf in London is a popular comedy horror about two friends and their encounter with werewolves.

PolyGram Pictures presents a Lycanthrope Films Limited production
An American Werewolf in London
starring David Naughton, Jenny Agutter, Griffin Dunne & John Woodvine
Original music by Elmer Bernstein · Executive producers Peter Guber & Jon Pete
Produced by George Folsey, Jr. · Written and directed by John Landis
PolyGram Pictures   "Meco's Impressions of An American Werewolf in London"
Marketed by PolyGram Records

1989 The first sighting of a wolflike creature known as the Beast of Bray Road, in Wisconsin.

GLOSSARY

CANNIBAL

A person who eats the flesh of other humans. Also, an animal that feeds on others of its own kind.

FOLK STORIES

Traditional stories told in particular regions of the world. They began as spoken word stories, and may have been very old by the time they were written down for the first time.

INVOLUNTARY WEREWOLF

A person who does not want to become a werewolf, but when a werewolf scratches or bites them, they are changed into one.

LYCANTHROPE

Another word for a werewolf. It comes from two Greek words—*lykos* meaning "wolf," and *anthropos* meaning "human."

MUSKET

A gun with a long barrel that fires a ball of lead.

PENTAGRAM

A star with five points, thought to have magical powers.

SHAPE-SHIFT

The ability of a werewolf to change its shape from its human form into its wolflike form, and then back again.

TRANSFORMATION

The process of changing a human into a werewolf.

VOLUNTARY WEREWOLF

A person who wants to become a werewolf.

WOLF BELT

A belt of wolfskin worn around the waist, which has the power to transform a person into a werewolf.

INDEX

American werewolves 14–15

Beast of Bray Road 15
Beast of Gévaudan 29
becoming a werewolf 8–9
bristles 13

cannibals 19
curing werewolves 25
cuts 13, 24, 28

destroying a werewolf 28–29
Diana, goddess of the Moon 25
double lives 4, 12

fairy tales 5, 11, 17
first werewolf 6–7
folk stories 4, 17, 29
forests 24
fur 8, 13

Greifswald 22–23
Grenier, Jean 26–27

howling 17
Hubert, St 25

imaginary werewolves 5
intelligence 20
involuntary werewolves 5, 9

Little Red Riding Hood 5, 10–11
lunatics 17
lycanthropes 7
Lycaon 6–7

meaning of "werewolf" 4
Moon 16–17, 24
Moon madness 17

pentagram 13
powers of werewolves 20–21
protection from werewolves 24–25

scratches 4, 9, 26
shape-shifters 4, 5, 8, 15, 16, 21

sight, werewolf's 21
silver 23, 24, 29
silver bullets 23, 29
smell, sense of 21
spells 9, 25
spotting a werewolf 12–13, 24
strength 19, 20
Stubbe, Peter 18–19

teeth 8, 12, 21
thirst 24
transformation process 9, 17, 21

voluntary werewolves 5, 8, 19

Weyer, Johann 27
wolf belts 9, 19
wolfsbane 25
wolves 11, 15, 17, 23, 25, 29

Zeus 6–7